World Class Manufacturing

Top Management's

Guide to
World Class
Manufacturing

FIRST EDITION

David W. Buker, Inc.

·BUKER·

Edited by Barbara Paddock, The Lowell Press, Inc., Kansas City, Missouri

Library of Congress Catalog Card Number 93-070637

ISBN: 0-932-84559-2

FIRST EDITION
First Printing 1993

©1993 by David W. Buker, Inc.

Printed in the United States of America by The Lowell Press, Inc.
Kansas City, Missouri

Contents

Preface

David W. Buker, Inc. has spanned three decades of operation and has offices on four continents. During our existence and our work throughout the world, there has been one constant. That constant has been our desire and our clients companies' desire for excellence in the total business enterprise.

This quest for excellence over the years has involved utilization of tools such as Total Quality (TQ), Just-In-Time (JIT), and Manufacturing Resource Planning (MRP II). With the implementation of each of these strategies and techniques, senior management has sought a sustainable, long-run competitive advantage. Today that desire is best expressed in the ideal of World Class Manufacturing. This book is a primer for the executive who would like to know more about World Class Manufacturing and how they can initiate the concepts in their business. This book is obviously not a substitute for the education process required to make the concepts of World Class Manufacturing a reality. Our experience has been that the only way to sustain a competitive advantage is to outpace the competitor's rate of organizational learning. It is our sincere hope that this book sparks that desire for learning.

The question and answer format utilized in this book is different from most others. The questions are not hypothetical. They are questions that we at David W. Buker, Inc. are continuously asked in our education classes and in our consulting with client companies. The book is intended to be read by manufacturing executives and used as a catalyst for discussion within senior management on the concepts of World Class Manufacturing

Best wishes on your journey to World Class Manufacturing.

Michael G. Tincker

President
David W. Buker, Inc.

CHAPTER ONE

World Class Manufacturing

1. What is World Class Manufacturing?

World Class Manufacturing is the term used to describe the very best manufacturers in the world. These World Class companies recognize the importance of manufacturing as a strategic weapon. World Class Manufacturing plays a central role in creating and sustaining customer satisfaction through the elements of quality, cost, flexibility, reliability and innovation.

Characteristics of World Class Manufacturing companies are:

1) *An ongoing company-wide education and training initiative for human resource development which allows everyone to actively participate in the improvement process.*

   The importance of education and training for all employees cannot be overemphasized. Studies have shown that World Class manufacturers provide a minimum of forty (40) hours of education and training per employee on an annualized basis. In today's business environment, the only long-term sustainable competitive advantage is organizational learning.

2) *Relentless pursuit of continuous improvement in all business activities.*

The management focus is on establishing operating performance measurements that drive the behaviors consistent with the goal of continuous improvement in both process and product. Measurements in place focus on rates of improvement.

3) *A dedication to developing a competitive advantage based upon superior product quality and service.*

The World Class company creates a level of customer satisfaction through being not only "easy to do business with," but by meeting and exceeding expectations. The term "customer delight" is an often-used expression when procuring products or services from a World Class manufacturer.

4) *Utilization of an integrated business system that links people and process.*

All business functions actively pursue a process of factory and business simplification, resulting in a systems integrative approach.

2. How do I get started on the Journey to World Class Manufacturing?

The one characteristic that stands out among World Class firms is a visible champion within the top management ranks. Someone in the senior management must provide the vision and leadership to guide the organization on the journey.

In the early 1980's one of the best methods for introducing the organization to World Class methods of operation was through studying successful companies. At that time examples of World Class Manufacturing were hard to find. Many executive teams went to Japan to witness firsthand the productivity and quality improvements being made there. Today visiting Japan is no longer necessary to learn about World Class Manufacturing.

Education should start with senior management creating a shared vision, consensus and commitment to World Class performance levels. This can be accomplished through attendance at courses on World Class Manufacturing, visiting companies achieving WCM status, reading books on the subject, and participating in professional societies dedicated to helping companies on their journey to World Class. (A listing of professional societies that can help on the World Class journey appears in the back of this book.)

3. Where does Manufacturing Resource Planning (MRP II) fit in?

Manufacturing Resource Planning or MRP II is a method for effectively planning all the resources of a manufacturing company. Over the last 20 years MRP II implementation has been for many companies their first concerted effort to significantly improve operating performance in the business.

However, it is important to understand that MRP II, even at Class A levels of performance, is not the same as World Class. Class A MRP II is defined as achieving 95 percent performance in all company functions. A Class A company is one with a management process that is in control, has achieved predictable performance and has a one plan process that all company functions work to. Class A does not necessarily ensure competitiveness, but only provides a formalization of the business which stabilizes the operation, allowing time to continuously improve operations.

4. Where does Just-In-Time fit in?

While Manufacturing Resource Planning (MRP II) pro-

3

vides a formal business process which operates in control, Just-In-Time (JIT) defines process improvement by focusing on simplification and elimination of waste of time and resources in the total business process.

Waste can be defined as those business activities which do not add value (cost-added). For most companies, these types of activities are institutionalized into the way the company does business. Another way to think of cost-added is the concept of work versus motion. Work is the value add, and cost add is motion. Our experience generally has been that 70 percent of the activities in a company are motion and 30 percent are work. In the World Class manufacturer these percentages are reversed. The World Class company has a 70 percent work ratio to a 30 percent motion ratio.

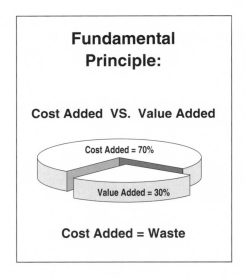

Just-In-Time focuses on improving the flow of material and information, and reduces the administrative and production cycle times. JIT can complement MRP II by allowing a company not only to be predictable, but highly flexible and responsive in its business processes.

5.   Where does Total Quality fit in?

Total Quality (TQ) and Just-In-Time (JIT) are closely linked. Each of these strategies emphasizes continuous process improvement, resulting in extremely high levels of precision, exactness and repeatability in both production and administrative processes.

Total Quality strives to reduce variation in business processes. It extends the continuous improvement process from raw material to the end user in the product chain. TQ encompasses the entire life cycle of a company's products from concept and product definition to end of life. It crosses all functional boundaries and involves people at all levels in the organization in a structured process of problem solving. TQ focuses on the customer, both internally and externally, to understand their needs completely and then to meet or exceed them with exceptional precision and exactness. This focus on precision, exactness and repeatability in all business processes is essential if a company is to achieve World Class levels of performance.

6.   How are MRP II, JIT and TQ different from World Class Manufacturing?

MRP II, JIT and TQ are all strategies that must be integrated for a company to achieve World Class performance. The degree of utilization varies from company to company, but elements of each will be in place in World Class companies. Another way to think of World Class Manufacturing is that its accomplishment is a result of many organized improvement efforts. MRP II, JIT and TQ are the foundation of the organized improvement efforts that companies use to achieve World Class levels of performance.

7.   What kind of results can I expect from activating a World Class Manufacturing initiative?

The results can be broken into two categories: direct results and by-product results. First, the direct results of the improvement processes.

Lead Time - 50-75 Percent Reduction

A lead time reduction of 50-75 percent applies to not only the manufacturing cycle time, but also from order entry to product shipment. To accomplish significant reduction in cycle or lead time, the focus is on elimination of cost-added activities.

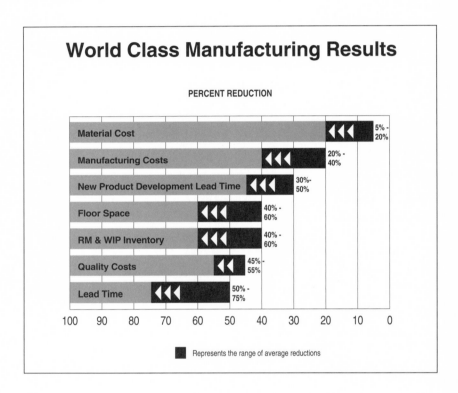

Quality Costs - 45-55 Percent Reduction

The reduction in the cost of quality by 45-55 percent is accomplished through a reduction in appraisal, and internal and external failure costs. Elimination of inspection of incoming material, in-process material, sorting finished product and fool-proofing processes that eliminate rework contribute to a reduction in defects.

6

Inventory - 40-60 Percent Reduction

The reduction in inventory may include not only in-process material, but raw material and finished goods. Reductions are attributable to collapsing the throughput time in the total business process, significantly improved quality and improved flexibility to respond to customer requirements.

Floor Space - 40-60 Percent Reduction

A 40-60 percent reduction in floor space pertains to the distance product travels during the manufacturing process. The preferred method of manufacture becomes one of a focus on flow and throughput, using concepts such as cellular manufacturing, group technology and continuous flow manufacturing. This method replaces the more traditional approach to manufacture by department, where the focus is on maximizing individual department efficiency.

New Product Development Lead Time - 30-50 Percent Reduction

With a business environment characterized by shorter product life cycles, a competitive advantage is achieved through time to market. Reducing new product development lead time enables more frequent product introduction and roll out of product performing to a slot in time.

Manufacturing Costs - 20-40 Percent Reduction

The reduction in manufacturing costs results from a management focus on process improvement throughout the business. Process improvements are achieved through elimination of non-value added activities, driving factory and business simplification. Reduction in manufacturing costs is a confirmation of quality improvements, cycle time reduction, reduced inventory levels and space utilized to manufacture.

Material Costs - 5-20 Percent Reduction

Material costs are reduced not by focusing on price but

7

on total costs. Approximately 40 percent of total cost of purchasing material from the supplier base is in non-price areas. Non-price areas are inspection of incoming material, storage of material, rework of material and excessive material handling before performing value-added activities.

The second category of results might be thought of as the by-product of the described improvements. The World Class company becomes the preferred supplier in world markets; the capital magnet in financial markets; the sought-after place of employment; and the business of choice by the community.

The long-term results are not only increased market share (10-20 percent is common) and profitability, but a culture of continuous improvement.

The Preferred Supplier in World Markets

Quality. Quality is first and the best. The product not only meets specifications, but it performs the desired function for the customer.

Reliability. The product has a long life and the customer knows that the product will "last forever."

Dependability. If something should go wrong with the product, the customer knows it will be made right quickly and without hassle.

Time To Market. World Class companies are in the marketplace first with new products which puts them first in the minds of the customer.

Customer Delight. Customers are not serviced or supported, they are delighted. The whole experience in doing business with World Class companies is delightful.

Technology. Products have all the latest technology the customer wants (or World Class companies want them to have).

Availability. The product is readily available or can be obtained in short order. No competitor gets product to the customer faster than World Class companies do.

World Markets. Product is available in any world market.

The Capital Magnet in World Financial Markets

If there is investment money available, the wise choice is to invest in the company. The World Class Company will attract capital from all parts of the world. With a substantial supply of capital, growth can be funded and resources kept up to date. Here are some investor considerations:

Return On Investment. Foremost in the investor's mind is how much money will be returned for the money put in. A healthy ROI is an indicator that the company is doing the exercises required to stay fit!

Profit. Certainly an attractive profit margin will help boost ROI and attract capital.

The Balance Sheet. The financial ratios associated with the balance sheet should be second to none. Possibly some radical thinking could be used in the balance sheet. Has anyone shown inventory as a liability and education as an asset?

Growth. A strong and steady growth rate of sales, profit, ROI, and earnings per share help attract capital.

Cost-Added vs. Value-Added Mindset. Each person in the business has an understanding of cost-added and can easily spot activities which add value and those that add cost. Each person works to eliminate waste every day. This mindset helps the business continually improve and be more profitable.

Benchmarking. The World Class company should know how it stacks up against competitors and those in similar industries. It is important to continuously improve and useful to know your relative position.

Business Processes. The World Class company has a business plan, sales plan, and a well-defined, robust top management planning process to review these plans on a regular basis, adjusting them in a timely manner. Operational and financial performance in all business areas are measured and reviewed monthly, weekly, and daily.

Management. Many investors will look only at the management team. If the right team is in place, most weaknesses in the business have a good chance of being corrected.

The Sought After Place of Employment

When a job opening exists, people flock to the World Class company, and once people are there, they want to stay. Here are some ideas of why World Class companies are such good places to work.

Investment in People. As a routine practice, the company educates people on new ideas and provides continual training for the assigned job. The investment in people provides return in the form of waste elimination and performance improvement.

Total Employee Involvement. All employees are involved in the improvement process, and problem solving is part of every person's daily activity.

Culture of Continuous Improvement. Every employee is excited about making unprecedented improvements at an unprecedented pace. It is not the single million-dollar solution, but the million one-dollar solutions that count!

Pay for Knowledge. Pay is awarded on knowledge gained, training completed, skills mastered, and experience. Seniority and vertical position in the business have little to do with pay. The opportunity to grow horizontally in the organization is real, and promotion is from within.

Profit Sharing. All employees share in the profits. The formula is simple and the dollar amounts are communicated at least monthly.

International Employees. If the business is to be truly World Class, then people from other parts of the world should be in the company helping it understand how to do business in world markets.

Innovation Encouraged. The opportunity to "try and fail" without employment risk has been provided. Try something. If it does not work, we know what not to do! Management approval has been eliminated or significantly simplified, and idea implementation is immediate.

Safety and Health. World Class companies take the necessary and appropriate steps to ensure that people can be on the job without risk of injury or danger to health. Training at all levels enables safety to occur.

Business of Choice by the Community

All facets of government (state, city, and local) and the general population of the community want to have World Class businesses located in their area. Our World Class company is preferred over any other business as the right one to have in the community. Here are some reasons why:

Environment. The company does not pollute; does not require hazardous materials for processes; and does not use materials that cause environmental problems.

Community Involvement. The World Class company actively participates in building a cultural base, develops the educational system, and serves with community action groups.

Local Suppliers. Raw materials, component parts and services are sourced locally to the fullest extent. Partnerships are built and new suppliers are developed whenever possible.

Stable Workforce. Large layoffs and frequent hiring spurts are not common. Job security and stability are objectives of management, and steady growth provides long-term employment opportunities.

Point of Technology Transfer. The company works actively with local universities to develop new technologies. Application for these technologies provides the means for transferring it to real production.

Professional Partner. Societies like APICS, AME, SME, IIE, ASQC and others provide educational forums and activities, and the World Class company provides financial support, members, plant tours, meeting facilities, and attendees for society activities.

Profitability. The company makes money which not only ensures the viability of the business, but is a dependable source of tax revenue for the community.

Community Investment. The company is willing to put cash, equipment, and in-kind gifts directly into the community. A good example is a business donating an equipped personal computer lab to a local high school.

8.   How long should it take to get results?

Results in selected initiatives can typically transpire in as little as 90 to 120 days. In the 90 to 120 day time frame, results are normally achieved on a pilot or product line basis. However, do not be misled. World Class is no quick fix. The world market is continuously changing, with new entrants challenging the established players. Only full recognition of this fact and acknowledgment that we must maintain pace is sufficient to guarantee competitiveness and, ultimately, survival.

Our experience has been that the pilot project pays for the initiative for the first 18 months and yields at least a 250 percent return on the investment. Over the long term, a bottom line impact of 10 percent of annual sales is not uncommon.

It is also important to identify the less tangible result. The World Class company is one that has created a structure to succeed and taps into its most valuable asset, its people. Developing a culture which challenges people to continuously improve the business is a long-term strategy.

CHAPTER TWO

Applying World Class Manufacturing to Your Business

1. Why is World Class Manufacturing important for my business?

Very few industries are not affected by global competition. With higher levels of competitiveness, it follows that the consumer will ultimately decide upon the products which meet their needs in the areas of product features, dependability, availability and overall value. No business can afford to stand still. If your company is successful and profitable, you can be certain that there is someone who is preparing to take all or part of your market share. In today's environment, it is no longer good enough to be better than the company down the street. We must meet and beat the best from anywhere in the world. We can no longer think that failure to make it in world markets will not affect us at home. The very opportunity we have to compete in world markets carries with it the explicit threat that the same opposition we experience overseas can indeed successfully prosper in our home markets. The bottom line is that World Class Manufacturing is the best way to ensure the survival and prosperity of your company.

Another important point is that pursuing World Class Manufacturing benefits the major stakeholders in the business—management, employees, shareholders and the community. Employees develop their skills, knowledge and productive abilities, shareholders receive a higher than normal rate of return on their investment, and the community benefits by having a business entity that creates jobs and produces product with an absolute minimum of waste.

2.   If World Class Manufacturing has so much potential to help my business, why don't I hear more about it?

World Class Manufacturing is being worked on by many companies today under many names. Some of the names include: Just-In-Time (JIT), Total Employee Involvement (TEI), Value-Added Manufacturing (VAM), Continuous Improvement (CI), Activity Based Management (ABM), Total Quality (TQ), and Manufacturing Resource Planning (MRP II). Each is an improvement vehicle which, when utilized properly, can yield significant improvements to the business. It is important to emphasize, however, that World Class is generally the result of pursuing not one but an integration of these strategies and philosophies.

In the past several years, World Class Manufacturing has been the subject of several books and executive seminars. Numerous informational vehicles have begun to spring up around the world to attempt to pull the best practices and experiences together into a cohesive package.

Do not be surprised if World Class Manufacturing becomes the descriptor of the emerging globally competitive manufacturer in the 1990's.

3.   Why do you call it World Class Manufacturing? Does it only apply to manufacturing?

The principal reason for calling it World Class Manufacturing is to emphasize the strategic importance of the manufacturing resource. The real strength for a manufacturer lies in its ability to add value in its manufacturing processes. For this reason, the term is used to describe the highest level of manufacturing performance.

It is important to note that all types of businesses—banks, hospitals, insurance companies and distribution companies—are utilizing World Class principles. What business isn't working to improve flexibility, responsiveness, timeliness, exactness, precision and repeatability to delight the customer?

Many of the concepts and tools defined in World Class originated in manufacturing companies. Some of the concepts go all the way back to Henry Ford's River Rouge plant in 1914. World Class Manufacturing can be achieved only from an integrated effort across all functions in these companies. Manufacturing companies are where the most examples of improved quality, lead time reduction, shorter product introduction cycles, etc., can be seen.

4.   Are there any risks involved?

Risks may be perceived at two levels: do nothing or do something.

1) Do nothing.

There is the primary risk, which is what might occur if we don't accept the challenge. This is a subjective assessment in the short term, but always remember that in the long run the marketplace—not us—will decide.

2) Do something.

There are certainly some issues that we must be fully aware of when embarking on a program. There are significant organizational and cultural changes that must and will occur, but we would not consider these threats, only opportunities. We see the risks if we visualize businesses evolving through a succession of phases, from "out-of-control" through "in-control" to "responsive" and finally "innovative." The risk occurs if we mistake our current level of competence or if we attempt to short-circuit the evolution and move directly from "out-of-control" to either "responsive" or "innovative." We must avoid the mistakes of the past where we made promises to our customers that we were incapable of supporting or demanded innovation that our processes were incapable of sustaining.

5. If my corporation has a number of divisions, does World Class Manufacturing apply to all divisions making different products?

Yes, World Class Manufacturing applies to all divisions of the company. It is a journey of continuous improvement. All divisions within the company carry the company name, contribute to (or detract from) the bottom line, and may even be integral parts of the same product chain. Although some divisions will improve faster than others, all of them should be progressing toward World Class. In fact, multi-division companies have an advantage to the extent that they can shorten the learning curve by helping each other.

6. What about a company making highly engineered product? Does World Class Manufacturing apply?

Yes, World Class Manufacturing does apply to highly engineered products. In fact, it is even more important to get it "right the first time" from the customer's and production's point of view. Since highly engineered products are usually one-of-a-kind, companies do not get a chance to do it again or recover any losses incurred. These companies need to closely link the customer needs with manufacturing and suppliers to simultaneously engineer product and process. Quality of design and design for manufacturing are prerequisites for achieving World Class Manufacturing in a highly engineered business.

17

7. What about a process industry where there is already an excellent flow? Does World Class Manufacturing apply?

Although pure process industries have good flow, it can and in many cases should be improved. There are also many manufacturing companies which consider themselves process rather than discrete but in reality are a combination of the two, and in some eyes are actually more batch oriented than process oriented. Regardless of the degree to which a business is process oriented, there are many opportunities to improve. Flow alone does not ensure World Class performance. For example, World Class process manufacturers are highly flexible and can compete with anyone for both large and small orders. They are the best at changeover of the line or process. Being World Class in process industries also means you have the highest yields, the most capable processes, the best safety record, the best delivery performance and the best distribution system. More importantly, a World Class process company is getting better in each of these areas on an ongoing basis.

8. What about a pharmaceutical business where changes require governmental approval? Does it apply there?

Absolutely. In fact, some of the principles of World Class Manufacturing comply with governmental requirements and are normal business practices. In the health care manufacturer, documentation, policies and procedures already exist, typically up-to-date and accurate, which are all part of World Class. What can be different for the pharmaceutical manufacturer revolves around employee involvement. Suggestions for improvement by the work force must have approval if it affects the process or product. However, in the office environment where there may be significant waste, improvements can be independently pursued.

9. How about a division with low labor, material and manufacturing costs? What might the benefits be?

Again, the opportunities may not all be in manufacturing. The primary focus could be in the administrative area. For example, the pilot initiative might be on flow and cycle time reduction through the order entry process.

Another example could be in an environment that is research and development oriented. One of the major issues might be time to market. Other issues might be how quickly the company can respond to customer demands and marketplace opportunities. Areas for improvement which could be focused on might include waste in the R & D process, which activities add cost, and how to make the entire process faster.

10. What is the best environment for working toward World Class Manufacturing? Is it a function of size or complexity of the business?

The best environment for World Class Manufacturing is an environment that is in a learning mode and is willing to embrace the inevitable change that accompanies the journey.

There are two types of companies best suited to begin the journey. One is obvious—the company in crisis. A company in trouble is typically receptive to new ideas and ways of doing things. Examples of companies that have been successful in turning their business around, returning to being the preeminent manufacturer in their market, are well documented. What is not as well documented are those that waited too long to recognize the trouble.

The second type of company that is normally successful is one where someone in senior management is personally committed to leading the effort. Championing the effort means having a vision of World Class Manufacturing, spending less time fire fighting and more time growing people. Executive management must rethink previous behaviors and attitudes and understand their role as the leaders of the change process.

19

CHAPTER THREE

Results of World Class Manufacturing

1. **I have been reading about company successes. Does the pursuit of improved technology yield these incredible benefits?**

For the Harvard Business Review, Morgan Stanley economist Stephen Roach analyzed U.S. productivity and information-technology investments. In his findings, the productivity of the information-technology worker has stayed even with rates from the 1960's, despite the fact investment in technology rose to six times more than 1960's figures. Similarly, MIT Economics Professor Ernst Bernott and Tufts University Assistant Professor Catherine J. Morrison analyzed high-tech investments by 20 U.S. manufacturing industries. As they wrote in Computer World:

> *... the payoff from investment in high-tech*
> *capital falls short of the costs.*

Clearly, investments in information-technology alone are not yielding the large benefits. Given these studies and others, you would think that the manufacturing industry would respond with dramatic measures to wrestle control of the bottom line from the insatiable appetite of information-technology. However, the response of industry continues to be to invest in more information-technology rather than rethinking business processes and procedures.

It has been our experience that only 10-25 percent of the benefits come from technology. The fundamental issue is changing the way we do business. Our studies also show that 70 percent of all business activities are cost-added. If we take 10, 20 or 30 percent of these activities and convert them to value-added, the bottom line benefits are enormous.

2. Will World Class Manufacturing give me and my company the tools to be a leader in my industry?

World Class Manufacturing practices will provide you the lowest costs, the fastest time to market, the best customer service and satisfaction, the highest quality, the shortest product lead time, the highest return on investment, and the most productive work force. These are the characteristics that make a company a leader in its industry. World Class principles encourage companies to simplify processes first and apply technology to what remains. Eliminating cost-added activities minimizes the need for automation. One company's senior executive tells everyone in the company that when it comes to automation, "... we must earn the right to automate." Earning the right to automate means that processes have been simplified with a repeatability, precision, and exactness that now makes automation possible.

However, it is important to understand that to be a leader in any industry, a company must be producing and marketing products that the marketplace wants. It is not enough to be able to come out with products quickly and of high quality. The company has to be a leader in innovation.

21

3. Will these concepts of World Class work outside the factory floor?

The basic principles of waste reduction, flexibility, responsiveness to customer needs, and product and process quality apply to the administrative areas of the business and any other department within the company. To illustrate this point, our experience is that companies in the service industry (insurance and hospitals) are applying the concepts of World Class Manufacturing just as readily as manufacturers. A recent study of insurance companies showed that actual processing time for a claim was under 15 minutes, but cycle time for the claim was four weeks (receipt of claim to respond to claim).

At one of our recent top management classes, a senior executive gave a perfect illustration of how the concepts apply outside the factory floor. The company recently mapped their process from order entry to shipment, detailing all of the activities in the business process to ship the product. To map the entire process required eight feet of paper. Seven and one-half feet involved taking the customer order and communicating the order to production. In other words, only six inches of the eight feet of the process mapping was producing the product. If you were going to start the continuous improvement process, would it be confined to just the factory floor in this company?

4. What would the major benefits be outside the manufacturing floor?

The benefits outside the factory floor are similar to what is found on the factory floor. Examples would be less rework (in most companies one-third of people's time is spent redoing what has already been done), quicker throughput from customer order to production, faster response from product design to production, and improved quality and elimination of waste throughout the total business process.

In World Class companies, responsiveness is key. Another way of putting it is that we are competing in time. Customers today want and expect accurate information, high quality and service quickly. The inability to provide quick response costs a company many times over. Studies have shown that regaining a customer once lost can be 10 times the cost of initially gaining that customer.

5. Do productivity improvements apply only to direct labor?

Absolutely not. Productivity today is defined as being much broader than its application to direct labor. In today's business environment only 5 to 15 percent of the cost is direct labor. Productivity improvements must be applied to the other areas of the business—indirect labor, office personnel, department managers, supervisors and top management. More importantly, productivity improvements are not just associated with people, but with all resources of the business. Companies are continuing to strive toward being more productive with inventory, receivables, plant and equipment. Labor is only one of the resources or inputs to the process of manufacturing.

When looking at the human resource, World Class manufacturers focus on making every mind in the business productive. Total employee involvement is critical to the continuous improvement process.

6. How do I get World Class Manufacturing going in the office?

The process is similar to the manufacturing operation formula for success. The process must start with education and leadership. The education must be for all office personnel regarding the concepts of World Class and how they apply to the office environment. Each person must be able to identify waste and understand the difference between cost-added and value-added activities. Management also needs to be willing to lead this activity.

23

As the education process begins, improvement teams are formed to identify specific problems and provide recommendations for improvements.

7. Explain the difference between value-added and cost-added activities.

To explain the difference between value-added and cost-added activities, it is important to look at the total business process consisting of only these two types of activities. An excellent definition of cost-added activities comes from a senior executive with whom we have consulted. This company's definition is:

> *Cost-added activities are those activities*
> *that, if the customer knew they went on,*
> *they would not willingly pay for them.*

Cost-added activities are typically institutionalized into the way the company does business. In other words, management and the work force look at these activities as an acceptable part of the process, referred to as a "cost of doing business." Consequently, time and energy are not spent on eliminating the activity, but fixes or work-arounds are developed to accommodate these variations in the process. Reorientation of the entire work force to identify cost-added activities and focus on their elimination is a major step on the World Class journey.

CHAPTER FOUR

The Costs

1. Give me some examples of cost-added activities.

If you go back to the definition of cost-added—"activities that, if the customer knew they went on, they would not willingly pay for them"—it is not hard to start to think of some examples. Some examples found in most businesses are:

- inspection of incoming material from suppliers
- storage of material and subsequent issuing of production material
- reworking material
- poor design resulting in engineering change notices
- business system transactions
- moving paperwork from one department to another
- moving material from one container to another

2. How would my company go about eliminating cost-added activities?

The first step to make sure that everyone is capable of

identifying cost-added activities. Obviously this occurs through the education process for all personnel. Each person is taught basic tools for problem-solving. Our recommendation for the initial management objective is to cut the waste or cost added by 50 percent. This means minor adjustments will not work, but rather a completely different approach must be tried. Improvements would not be superficial, but a fundamental change in the way the work is accomplished is required. Next, cut it in half again, providing for a 75 percent improvement. Then make it 10 percent of what it originally was.

3 Step Rule For Reducing Waste

STEPS	REDUCTION
1. REDUCED BY 50%	**50%**
2. REDUCED BY 50% AGAIN	**75%**
3. MAKE IT 10% OF WHAT IT WAS	**90%**

A good example might be in the area of quality of material output from a given work center. Step One, cut it in half, let's say from 1000 parts per million defect to 500 parts per million. Step Two, cut it to 250 defects and then 10 percent of the original number of defects or 100.

The improvement process does not stop there. At this point in time the group involved in the improvement process continues reducing the number of defects. It is important to note that when looking for waste or cost added activities, everyone must understand that people are not cost-added, but the activities they are engaged in are.

3. What are the costs associated with a World Class initiative?

The costs associated with achieving World Class today can be broken into a number of categories such as cost of education, cost of employee's time and cost of equipment. Work force education is one cost. Education of the work force could include education through vehicles such as seminars, video-based education, involvement with professional organizations, and visiting other companies to learn best practices.

Another area of cost is people's time. This is time spent away from their normal jobs. The time for the work force to be engaged in improvement activities is not an out-of-pocket cost but a reallocation of the work force. Also, equipment purchases for the factory and office can be incurred.

World Class companies do not view education as a cost. It is viewed as an investment with a specific return on the investment.

4. What about the cost of education and how do we conduct the education process?

The education process is broken into three levels or steps.

The first step in the education process is senior management. This step is normally conducted through attendance at a top management course dealing with the principles of World Class Manufacturing, where senior management's role in the initiative is defined along with the key measurements to drive the continuous improvement effort and the steps to success. The top management education is designed to develop a consensus and common understanding at the senior management level.

The second step in the education process is the education for the operating management. Operating management education is best conducted through in-house, application-oriented education for department managers, key staff/support, and first-line supervision. Each session of in-house education should be cross-functional, providing a total process approach or orientation to the business. The operating management education is normally started approximately 30 days after the top management education.

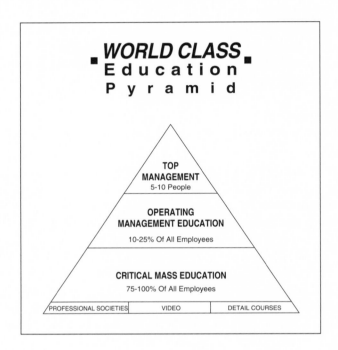

The third step in the education process is the education for the critical mass. This education is in the form of detailed courses in topics such as inventory accuracy, setup reduction, and basic problem solving. Today more and more companies are utilizing video-based education to assist in the education initiative.

Regarding the costs of education, our surveys and experiences with World Class manufacturers are that education is approximately 15 percent of the total cost of the improvement effort.

5. I've heard that practically everyone must be educated in my company. How do we do it?

In the World Class manufacturer everyone receives education and training. Senior management many times is surprised at the idea of educating everyone. What we normally tell executive management is, "Pull out a sheet of paper and write down the names of employees that do not need to know anything about continuous improvement." The answer is obvious. If continuous improvement is important for all functions in the business, everyone needs to be involved. Remember, the World Class manufacturer looks at education with a specific return on investment (ROI). Also, in Chapter 3 we talked about making every mind in the business productive through the idea of total employee involvement.

How are companies educating everyone? Well, one of the cost-effective methods is the use of video-based education. Companies are using video in what we would call a three-step process. Step one is to lead a small group (8 to 10 people) through the video subject matter. The video is normally 12 to 15 minutes and presents information and concepts. Step two is a work exercise. There is always a higher level of comprehension when one is given a chance to practice what has been learned. Step three, possibly the most important, is the discussion, the application of, "How does this apply to my business and, more importantly, how do we make it happen in my company?" This provides the closure on the learning experience. The video thus is used as a catalyst in bringing people together in a forum for the exchange of ideas to develop the communication, teamwork and ownership to develop action plans to improve the business. We like to think of it as a focused business meeting approach.

6. What about in-plant education? Why should I do it for some of my people?

In-plant education has some important advantages and is accomplished in two ways: one, have professional instructors come into your facility, and two, use company personnel to do it.

The outside professional education resource is applicable when the education objectives are vision, outside experience, other companies' perspectives, specific methodology and compact timing (one to three day format). Doing inplant, application-oriented education in this manner normally reduces the time frame six months over sending people to outside courses and is obviously more cost-effective.

Company people conduct sessions when the objectives are company application, team-building, project ownership and specific action plans for improvement. To be effective internal educators, proper course ware is required and the educator should be a trained facilitator (not necessarily a subject matter expert). These sessions are done a few hours per week over a long period of time. The idea is to have an ongoing focus on improvement activities.

7. What about continuing education? What do World Class manufacturers do?

As part of the education plan, World Class Manufacturing companies encourage several continuing education activities:

1) *Develop and maintain a company library on the subject matter.*

2) *Encourage and fund professional society memberships.*

3) *Financially reward successful professional certification.*

4) *Conduct required educational activities for new employees.*

5) *Attend national conferences annually.*

6) *Routinely visit other businesses.*

A word about World Class manufacturers on continuing education is important here. Our surveys tell us that each of them has minimum requirements of 40 hours of education per employee on an annualized basis.

8. What about outside guidance? Why should I use it?

The purpose of using outside guidance is to shorten the time frame of achieving benefits in the World Class initiative. Consultants can bring their experiences to bear, assisting you through technical issues and working with improvement teams and senior management by helping to set objectives and reviewing performance.

Consultants are best used when the company does not look to them to implement the programs. The people in the business need to do the work. Our recommendation is for the consultant to visit the business every four to six weeks in two-day segments. This allows the consultant to operate as a different set of eyes or with an outsider's perspective on the business. Success does not result when the consultant is in your company on a daily basis, actively participating and, in effect, doing the tasks of improvement.

9. Will I need new computer systems to start working toward World Class Manufacturing?

New computer systems are not required to begin the World Class initiative. Processes must be defined, with improvements to the process looked at first. Too often companies purchase new computer systems and implement them over their existing operations. Then, they wonder why significant improvement does not occur. Quite often the problem is not the existing computer systems. Remember, World Class manufacturers have a passion for factory and business simplification and consistently strive to reduce cost-added activities rather than automate them.

If new systems are required, requirements must be first defined. This is why education is so important. Company management must first be educated about the changes which typically transpire on the journey to World Class.

CHAPTER FIVE

The Senior Manager's Role

1. What is different about managing in a World Class Manufacturing company?

In a World Class company, there is clearly one set of objectives for the business functions. Barriers between functions are eliminated, operating facts are the basis of communication and trust exists between departments. Responsibilities and accountabilities are defined and agreed upon, which allows decisions to be made at the lowest possible level in the organization, and each employee is involved in the improvement process. The culture is one of active risk-taking and allowing people to make mistakes.

The focus of performance measurements in the operation is on rates of improvement. Traditional measures such as indirect to direct labor ratios, manufacturing efficiency, purchase price variance and overhead absorption, no longer are major issues and are not measured.

The World Class manufacturer sharply contrasts with the traditional company where each department has its own objectives and the overall company objectives are not clear. In the traditional environment, all decisions are made at a high level and only "professionals" are involved with making the business better.

32

2. Will we have different objectives in a World Class manufacturer than we have had before?

The focus is on longer term objectives. In many companies today, management is very short-term focused. They are interested in this month's financials and will do what it takes to make it happen. In this environment, everyone is rewarded and praised for reacting. The problem with this mode of operation is that unusually high costs are incurred and, at the same time, largely hidden.

World Class company managers look for the long-term benefit and payoff. They know an investment in people and planning now will help avoid costs and problems in the future. Each employee becomes a problem-solver. Short-term goals remain important, but not at the expense of long-term objectives.

3. How might my role as a senior manager change? Give me some examples.

The executive must make a personal commitment to World Class and Total Quality throughout the organization. This commitment must be highly visible.

The chief executive's personal commitment must be continuously reinforced during the early stages of the process. Senior managers, to get the initiative underway, should:

1) *Personally lead their management teams through the initial phases of education.*

2) *Take an active role in competitive analysis and benchmarking.*

3) *Require cost of poor quality data be collected and communicated.*

4) *Require customer satisfaction (internal and external) data be compiled and utilized.*

5) *Support the reallocation of the work force to problem solving.*

33

6) *Be visible in the operation, talking about improvement at all levels.*

7) *Put an emphasis on process improvement measures rather than results measures.*

Only senior managers can create an environment which fosters continuous improvement by enlisting the efforts of all people at all levels in the organization. This leadership effort is never-ending.

4. What kind of actions should I be taking to get the effort underway?

Some behaviors and actions to facilitate the improvement process are:

1) *Ensure that the critical resource—people's time—is made available to work on the improvement process.*

2) *Eliminate corporate and functional barriers to improvement. Only senior management can push these obstacles out of the way.*

3) *Flatten the organization's structure. Flat organizations result in better communication, greater flexibility and lower total cost.*

4) *Establish cross-functional goals.*

5) *Treat human resources as a strategic issue.*

6) *Demand linear performance in the execution of all plans.*

7) *Get to know your customers, suppliers and employees.*

8) *Be the champion of change.*

9) *Set improvement goals and objectives and effectively communicate them to the organization.*

5. Why is top management commitment and involvement so important in the World Class Manufacturing initiative?

Historically for many companies there have been numerous improvement initiatives that are critical initially but, due to lack of long-term commitment, become "projects of the month."

Commitment means company-wide communication and direct involvement of management at all levels. It means devoting resources, both people and equipment, to improving the business process. Regular involvement and the establishment of challenging goals for improvement teams are essential. It also means being dedicated to the continuous development of people through education.

6. What kind of problems can I expect to encounter?

The major problems that companies encounter in their World Class initiative are most frequently people related rather than technically related. For instance, resistance from senior staff could occur because they are being asked to change the very behaviors that got them where they currently are in the organizational hierarchy. Another example is the conflict which results when traditional financial performance measurements become subordinate to process improvement measurements.

More serious is a reluctance by certain segments of the organization to believe the company is really serious about the initiative. There may be the attitude of, "We have seen these types of programs come and go before." Many people will probably have to be shown. Finally, mid-level managers may block the process because of the significant change some of their jobs may undergo. A good example of the change in job characteristics involves first-line supervision. The supervisor's job moves from one of telling people what to do to a role of coach and facilitator.

7. How do companies keep all levels of the organization motivated in the World Class Manufacturing effort?

The three keys in keeping people motivated are education, individual and group ownership of the improvement process, and recognition for improvements attempted, be they successful or unsuccessful.

The education process is typically the first exposure to World Class concepts for the vast majority of the employees in the company. Providing the vision of where the company intends to go in the future and each person's role in the journey is extremely motivating for most employees. In Chapter 4 we talked about the three steps in the education process to educate 100 percent of the organization.

The individual and group ownership of the improvement process is handled through the activation of small groups which focus on solving specific, defined problems. It is also important to understand that in creating ownership, the work force must have the responsibility and authority to implement improvements. This does not mean 16 signatures for every $50 improvement idea. World Class companies have very few impediments to implementation of improvements. In fact, it is senior management's job to remove the impediments.

Management recognition of work force improvements is also a critical factor in continuous motivation. Recognition does not always have to be monetary. We have seen everything from pizza for the group and tickets to a sporting event, to providing the opportunity for the improvement teams to present their ideas to senior management.

8. How can I consistently communicate to the organization my support for the effort?

First and foremost, allow time for the small groups to work on improvements. Let's take an example. We recently conducted an in-plant course for a company, and the discussion turned to the subject of allowing time for the improvement teams to work on problems. A company executive stated that the teams were going to be allowed, after their regular workday, to work on improvements. I might add, they were going to be paid overtime! Now what is the message for those involved? The activity is being communicated as an addition to the regular job, therefore, the improvement process is not ongoing. It has more of a project status. Too often management has viewed time allowed during the regular workday devoted to problem solving as non-productive, particularly when talking about the hourly work force. This obviously means that only when product is made, "productive time," can the company be making money.

The World Class manufacturer makes improvement activities not an addition to the regular work but a part of the regular work.

CHAPTER SIX

What Must be Done to Successfully Achieve World Class Manufacturing

1. **There certainly are companies that have not achieved the results you identified. What are the pitfalls?**

The pitfalls really start with education or the lack of it. Too many companies look for technology (new equipment or computer systems) to generate significant business improvement. That is a little like giving a golfer a new set of golf clubs and expecting to see significant improvement. It just does not happen. Companies that are the most successful in their World Class efforts understand that they are trying to raise the technical competence throughout the entire organization. One general manager recently told us, "Every worker is an industrial engineer." What the general manager meant was that the company was trying to teach each person the basic problem-solving skills necessary to identify and solve core problems.

A second major pitfall is too often management looks at

World Class as a quick fix or another program. A program implies that there is a beginning and an end. World Class manufacturers are telling us that, rather than a quick fix, World Class is a forever commitment to the elimination of waste in the total business process.

Another major pitfall involves people engaged in the improvement process. When a company starts making 25, 30, 50 or 75 percent improvement in a process, the process is going to require fewer people to manage and operate. The solution cannot be to lay off the people who have made the significant improvements because they are no longer needed. Many companies have done exactly that! Consequently, for self-preservation people halfheartedly approach additional improvements. Management's challenge is to utilize these people in other value-added activities. For example, many World Class manufacturers today utilize manufacturing personnel in pre-sales work or engage them in improvement activities in supplier operations. The objective is to use those people to share with the customer (and associated businesses) in the improvements they have made in their own business.

2.   What are the steps to success?

There are five key steps to success for any company embarking on the journey to World Class Manufacturing.

Step 1) *Education*

The education process consists of three levels — top management, operating management and critical mass education. (Refer to Chapter 4 for a more detailed explanation of the education process.) The education process must encompass everyone in the organization and start with senior management. Senior management must have a common vision and understanding. As a team, they must reach a consensus on how to begin the initiative. Education normally takes a number of formats. For example, seminars, video-based education and books are used. Often plant visits to other high performance businesses provide an excellent learning experience and build firsthand awareness of improvement.

Step 2) *Company Assessment*

The company assessment conducted by the internal management determines and prioritizes the areas of improvement for the business and provides management with a quantification of the benefits by making the opportunities a reality.

Step 3) *Company Action Plan*

After the company has addressed the opportunities of the World Class initiative, an action plan is developed. This action plan defines the scope of activities (a vision statement), specific tasks, objectives and benchmarks, time frames and responsibilities to improve the performance to desired World Class levels.

Step 4) *Cross-Functional Team*

A cross-functional team must be created to activate the World Class effort. The team should have representation from each area of the business. Multi-department representation is necessary to reflect the changes to the total business operation. This representation would include Sales, Manufacturing, Engineering, Logistics, Finance, Quality, Human Resources, Information Systems and Planning. A leader from senior management must be responsible for the team's performance and drive the initiative throughout the organization.

The tasks of the cross-functional team are: the education of the organization, development of an action plan, and leading the small groups engaged to improved performance in each area. The team should meet on a weekly basis during the beginning stages of the initiative and on a regular basis thereafter.

Step 5) **Performance Measurement**

Beginning the journey to World Class requires activating a habit of continuous improvement throughout the business enterprise. The purpose of performance measurement is to measure the rate of improvement in the critical areas of quality, cost, flexibility, reliability and innovation.

These five areas and the detailed measures and benchmarks are outlined in the Appendix of this book.

3. If continuous improvement is really continuous, how do I know that we are making ongoing progress?

The only way to know if progress is being made toward continuous improvement is to use tangible measures of both the process and the results. For example, planning and scheduling elements could be measured on percent actual performance to planned performance. There are also numerous baseline measurements which should be employed. Examples of these measurements would include: manufacturing and total business cycle time, number of capable machines, number of certified suppliers, first pass yield and number of suggestions implemented by the improvement teams. These baseline measurements are not measured as percent performance to plan, but are measured in terms of rates of improvement using previous performance as the baseline.

4. How do I get the hourly work force involved in the problem solving and continuous improvement initiative?

The most effective method to involve the hourly work force is through the use of small group improvement activities (SGIA). Small group improvement activities are performed by groups of less than 10 people which address specific performance problem areas. For example, in a company that has extensive changeover times in their process or long setups on a particular piece of equipment, the objective is to see significant reduction in the time required to accomplish the changeover. The objective might be to reduce the changeover time by 50 percent in the next 90 days. To achieve that goal, management would activate a small group consisting of hourly personnel, Maintenance, Engineering, Material Handling, Supervision and Quality to together work on the changeover.

There are two very important points about the small groups activated to improve the performance in an area. The teams must be educated and skilled in the use of basic problem-solving tools such as cause and effect diagrams, story boarding, five-why diagrams and Pareto analysis. The second important point is that there is recognition and reward for the teams. One of the most effective methods of recognition is for senior management to take the time to participate in the small group meetings and review progress with them. This activity sends a clear message throughout the organization of the commitment and involvement of management and the importance of the groups' effort, and recognizes their activities.

5. How do I avoid upsetting the company and running the risk of getting into serious trouble at the beginning of the initiative?

The trap that many companies fall into is having too many individual project initiatives going at the same time. Company employees begin to view each project as the "flavor of the month" or program of the month. We meet companies today working simultaneously on ISO 9000 certification, new product introduction, Just In Time (JIT), Manufacturing Resource Planning (MRP II), Total Quality (TQ) and a new business systems implementation. All of these may be important strategically for the company long-term. However, the problem is that each project is communicated to operating management as "the" priority. It is not humanly possible to do them all at once. Often times these tasks are misunderstood and seem to be in conflict, when in fact they are not. The conflict arises when all projects are competing for similar and limited resources. The operating management becomes frustrated because, depending upon whom they talk to at the senior management level (each is pushing their own program) and which day of the week it is, there is a different priority.

It is senior management's role to sort out which of these tools and techniques (MRP II, JIT, TQ, ISO 9000) will be activated and the priority, based on opportunity available, in applying each of the elements of these strategies. This again relates directly to the education process and its importance. As we mentioned before, a consensus needs to be developed through senior management education. This includes not only the belief that World Class Manufacturing is a priority, but also how the company plans to approach the effort, that the resources required are made available, and that all members of senior management are committed to active involvement as a united team.

CHAPTER SEVEN

Getting Started

1. Who should head up the World Class Manufacturing initiative?

Every successful World Class Manufacturing journey
has a top management champion. This should be the company chief executive officer. Companies that are successful in
their World Class efforts have all company functions
involved in the effort. The only position that cuts across all
functional areas of the business is at the top. It is important
that the person in charge of the business provide the leadership, support, objectives and vision to the organization.

We would also recommend that there is a coordinator
for the effort reporting to the company chief executive. The
coordinator of the World Class Manufacturing initiative
would have several responsibilities and is generally a full-
time position. The responsibilities include conduct and coordinate educational activities, involvement and coordination
of spin-off task forces whose charter it is to address problem
performance areas, development of the World Class Manufacturing plan, and reporting progress and coordinate activities with the executive steering committee.

The executive steering committee is made up of the chief executive and the executive staff. The committee typically meets at least on a monthly basis to review progress. This review normally takes two formats: a review of the status of the overall plan and an analysis of the rate of improvement in the key performance measurements—quality, cost, flexibility, reliability and innovation.

2. What is the role of the World Class Manufacturing plan?

Not dissimilar to a road map, the World Class Manufacturing plan is the document that outlines the objectives as defined by senior management and the activities and responsibilities to achieve these objectives.

The plan is helpful in providing:

1) *the vision of World Class Manufacturing through a mission statement. It is the mission statement which provides the charter for all improvement activities.*

2) *a prioritized listing of objectives that must be accomplished to achieve World Class Manufacturing. Responsibilities are assigned and time frames are defined for each objective.*

For each objective, there exists a target statement of the specific improvement activities to be accomplished to achieve the World Class Manufacturing objectives. The person responsible then activates the spin-off task forces or small group improvement activities (SGIA) to attack each targeted area.

The World Class Manufacturing plan is in a continuous state of review and revision. Weekly reviews of the small group improvement activities occur, with monthly review at the executive management level.

3. What is the frequency of review and who should be involved?

As previously mentioned, the senior management level review must be done at least monthly. However, senior management should not be concerned if it becomes necessary to meet more frequently. During the initial stages of the effort, senior management could be involved in additional education such as video-based education. In the early stages of this process, it is not uncommon for management to meet two to three times per week for one to one and a half hours.

The senior management review would involve the chief executive, the executive staff and the World Class Manufacturing coordinator. There also is a review at the operating management level that is led by the World Class coordinator and includes the cross-functional team involved in the improvement effort with focus on achievement of the activities in the plan.

4.   If a company is committing itself to World Class Manufacturing, does it start the initiative throughout the entire business?

It depends on the particular piece of the initiative and on the size of the company. Pieces of the initiative may include MRP II, JIT or Total Quality, and the company may be one plant of 300 people or have dozens of plants of varying sizes throughout the world.

As a general rule, the smaller the plant size the more can be done at once. If control via MRP II is the issue, it generally needs to be done throughout the plant. If JIT or TQ are the issues, they can be more readily piloted in smaller areas and allowed to grow into the total business over time. In very large companies each plant may have its own World Class Manufacturing timetable to suit its particular level of understanding and local issues.

We find that successful World Class Manufacturing companies do not use the "big bang theory" and become World Class overnight. Rather, World Class Manufacturing seeds were sown, cared for continuously and allowed to flourish. No shortcuts, no quick fixes, no miracles. Just good, fundamental, steady progress in the right direction. With this basic foundation, the World Class Manufacturing initiative spreads quickly to' other parts of the business.

However, when a World Class Manufacturing initiative is started, everyone should know the macro plan. If we are going to pilot certain areas in setup reduction techniques over the next three months, then let everyone know. Tell them that their turn is coming and allow them to learn from the pilot group's experience. If MRP II is to be implemented in one plant of one division, use it as a learning experience for all other plants and let them know the corporate intent for their involvement.

The important point is to have an overall macro plan for the World Class Manufacturing initiative that is well thought out and communicated to all employees.

5. How can I measure progress of the small group improvement activity (SGIA) teams?

SGIA teams should have specific direction from management and a well defined project to work on. Objectives and goals should be agreed upon between management and the SGIA team. The objective may be to reduce setup time on Machine No. 105. The goal may be to make a 50 percent reduction in three months.

Once objectives and goals are established, performance measurements can be put in place. In this example, performance could be measured by the percentage of time spent on setup activity or the number of setups categorized by time interval: 0-10 minutes, 10-30 minutes, 30-60 minutes, over 60 minutes. Each SGIA team should clearly understand the performance measurement.

Performance is reviewed in two ways. First, measurements should be posted very visibly in the workplace. Large white boards and markers are wonderful display tools. Second, each SGIA team should have the opportunity to

47

address top management monthly to present progress and performance.

6. How do we measure our performance in the process of striving for World Class Manufacturing?

Because a World Class Manufacturing effort is made up of many improvement activities being carried on throughout the company, a methodology to track progress must be established. This tracking method should consist of an ongoing posting of improvements compared to the current norms of operations. Since the improvements themselves become standardized into a new norm of operation, it is the ongoing rate of improvement which is of interest to management.

Periodic management reviews with individual small group improvement activity (SGIA) teams provide opportunities to hear a presentation summarizing the improvements achieved. These reviews provide the management an opportunity to reassess the SGIA guidelines and recognize results and the teams responsible for the improvements.

Performance Measurements for World Class Manufacturing

Definition of World Class Manufacturing

The term "World Class Manufacturing" is used to define the very best manufacturing companies worldwide. World Class companies are the leading (best of class) providers of the products and services in the markets they serve. Becoming a World Class Manufacturer results in becoming:

1) *The preferred supplier in world markets.*
2) *The capital magnet in financial markets.*
3) *The sought-after place of employment.*
4) *The business of choice by the community.*

The World Class Manufacturer recognizes the importance of manufacturing as a strategic weapon and is committed to continued business excellence. Manufacturing plays a central role in creating and sustaining customer satisfaction through the elements of quality, cost, flexibility, reliability and innovation.

Characteristics of World Class Manufacturing

1) *An ongoing company-wide education and training initiative for human resource development which allows everyone to actively participate in the improvement process.*

2) *Relentless pursuit of continuous improvement in all business activities.*

3) *A dedication to developing a competitive advantage based upon superior product quality and service.*

4) *Utilization of an integrated business system that links people and process.*

Measurements of World Class Manufacturing

In World Class manufacturers the focus is on continuous improvement. Measurements in place should therefore activate improvements. Management evaluates the measurement process based upon the rate of improvement. The measurements are designed to drive the improvement process in the critical elements of quality, cost, flexibility, reliability and innovation, the measurements we at David W. Buker, Inc. have seen and recommend for companies striving for World Class levels.

Quality

1) Percent reduction in total cost of quality.

2) Percent reduction in defects.

3) Percent of certified suppliers.

4) Percent reduction in supplier base.

5) Percent reduction in time between defect occurrence, detection and correction.

Cost

1) Percent increase in inventory turnover.

2) Percent reduction in data transactions.

50

3) Percent increase in materials shipped to point of use by supplier.

4) Percent increase in dollars of output per employee.

5) Percent reduction in floor space utilized.

Flexibility

1) Percent reduction in cycle time.

2) Percent reduction in setup time.

3) Percent reduction in lot/batch size.

4) Percent increase in number of jobs mastered per employee.

5) Percent increase in common materials used per product.

Reliability

1) Percent increase of process capable equipment.

2) Percent increase in overall equipment effectiveness.

3) Percent reduction in product or service warranty costs.

4) Percent reduction in engineering changes.

5) Percent increase in on-time delivery.

Innovation

1) Percent reduction in new product introduction lead time.

2) Percent increase in new product sales revenue as a percent of total sales revenue.

3) Percent increase in number of new patents granted.

4) Customer perception of the company as a leader in innovation.

5) Percent of management time spent on leading or fostering innovation.

How To Measure

Quality

1) Percent reduction in total cost of quality.

The reduction in total cost of quality would be measured on a monthly basis and typically is displayed in graph format. The elements of cost of quality measured are: prevention, appraisal, internal failure and external failure. These four elements are measured monthly as a percent of sales.

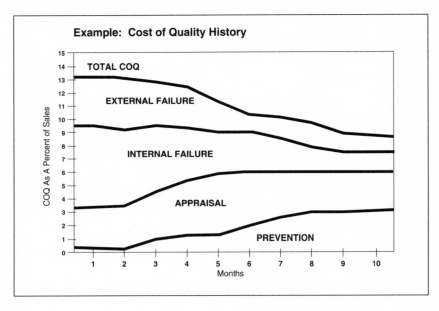

2) *Percent reduction in defects.*

The reduction in defects is measured in parts per million. The measurement is defects per unit relative to the number of opportunities possible for defects to occur. Reduction in defects is measured weekly and monthly. Normally this is displayed on a trend chart and is 1 million divided by total opportunities times the number of defects.

Example: **100 Board Assemblies Produced**
X 100 Components Per Board

10,000 Opportunites for Defects

10 Defects Occur

$$\frac{\text{Parts Per}}{\text{Million}} = \left(\frac{1,000,000}{10,000 \text{ Opportunities}} \right) \text{ X 10 Defects} = 1,000$$

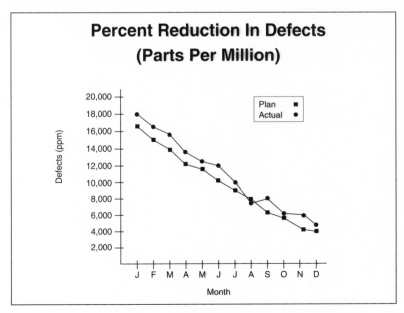

Percent Reduction In Defects (Parts Per Million)

53

3) *Percent of certified suppliers.*

Certified suppliers require, at the minimum, supplier's process has been certified to the point that there is no incoming material inspection required. Many companies working on certification certify by individual part rather than source of the part. Whichever method is used, data should be displayed on a trend line and reviewed monthly and appropriate actions taken.

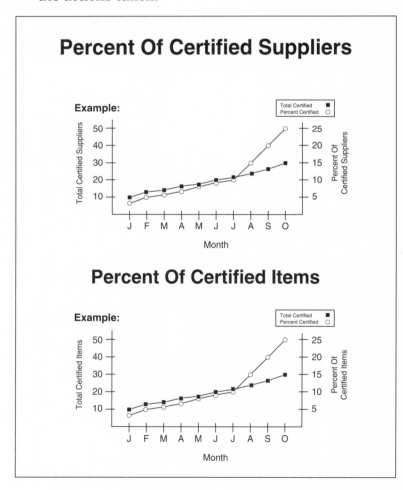

4) *Percent reduction in supplier base.*

This measurement is utilized to review improvements in quality of source of supplier. The supplier base typically is reduced by rewarding those sources that continuously improve quality, reduce lead time, improve on-time performance and supply materials that can be delivered to the point of use. The measurement is monthly and displayed as a trend line.

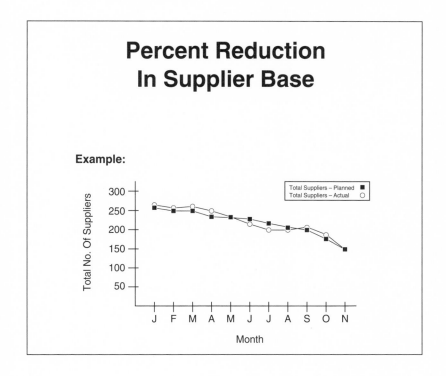

5) *Percent reduction in time between defect occurrence, detection and correction.*

There are actually three measurements: defect occurrence, defect detection and defect correction. This could be measured by way of a chart located in each work area with time horizontally displayed and defects vertically displayed. Operators would record time of occurrence, detection and correction. Results are summarized weekly and monthly.

Percent Reduction In Time Between Defect, Occurrences, Detection and Correction

Example: _____   Date: _____

Shift: _____

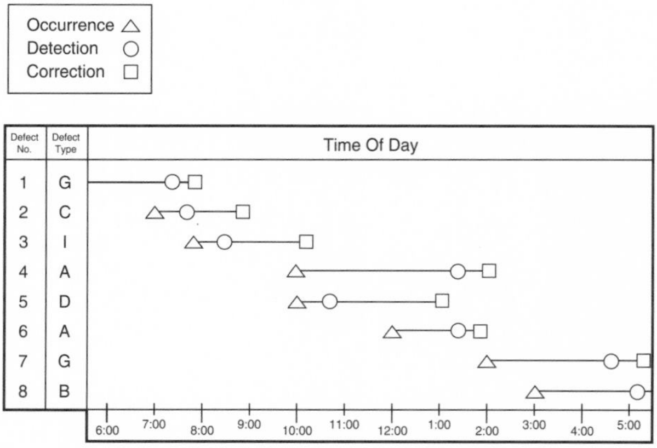

Occurrence △
Detection ○
Correction □

Defect No.	Defect Type	Time Of Day	Elapsed Time (Minutes) △—○	○—□	△—□
1	G				
2	C		110	15	125
3	I		30	30	60
4	A		90	45	135
5	D		130	20	150
6	A		15	60	75
7	G		30	5	35
8	B		150	30	180
		6:00 7:00 8:00 9:00 10:00 11:00 12:00 1:00 2:00 3:00 4:00 5:00	135	20	155

Total Elapsed Time	690	225	915
Average Elapsed Time	86	28	114

Cost

1) Percent increase in inventory turnover.

Inventory turnover is looked at as a measure of material throughput. The measurement is completed by compiling the annualized cost of sales and dividing it by current total inventory. Turnover is measured monthly and displayed on a trend line. Raw material and work in process can be measured separately from finished goods inventory.

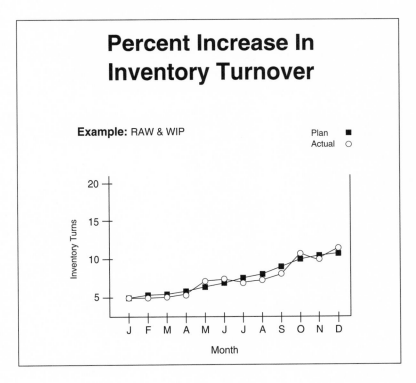

57

2) Percent reduction in data transactions.

Data transactions are considered one of the key wastes in the business process and should be minimized. The measurement should be by product line and measure transactions such as labor and inventory movement. The measurement should be against a baseline of business activity, such as total units produced. This measurement is monthly for the product line and is displayed on a trend line.

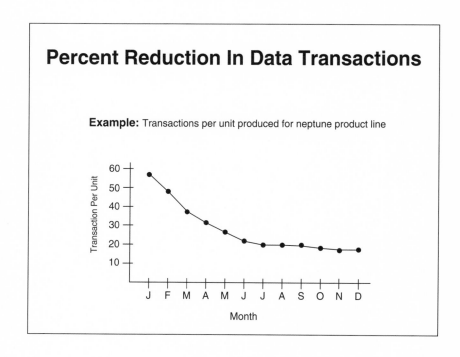

Percent Reduction In Data Transactions

Example: Transactions per unit produced for neptune product line

3) *Percent increase in materials shipped to point of use by supplier.*

Companies need to shorten the time to process incoming materials. Activities such as incoming inspection, material movement and taking material out of the shipping container to be put in another container suitable to the manufacturing process are cost-added. The measurement tracks by supplier the percent of materials that are able to be shipped directly to work-in-process. A trend line is used on a monthly basis to display the information.

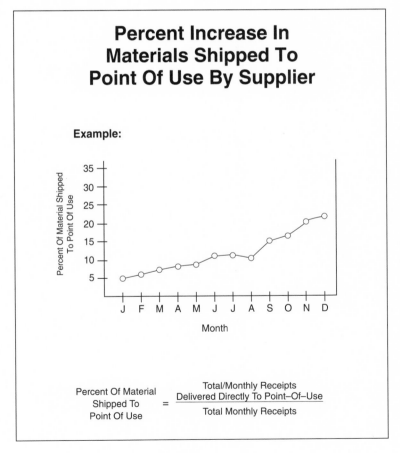

Percent Increase In Materials Shipped To Point Of Use By Supplier

4) *Percent increase in dollars of product output per employee.*

The measurement is a measure of productivity. It determines how effectively people and resources are being used in the production of the product. The calculation would be annualized sales divided by total number of employees. This should be measured monthly and displayed using trend lines.

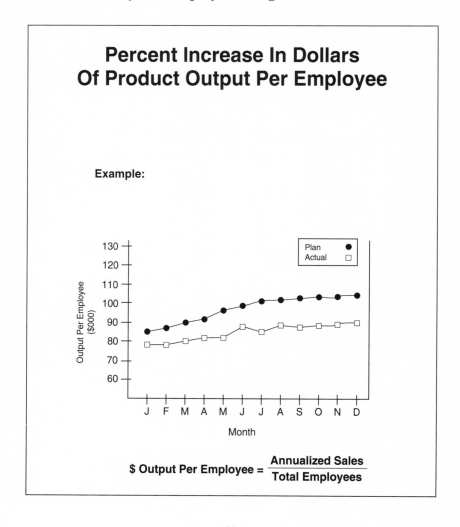

Percent Increase In Dollars Of Product Output Per Employee

Example:

$$\$ \text{ Output Per Employee} = \frac{\text{Annualized Sales}}{\text{Total Employees}}$$

5) *Percent reduction in floor space utilized.*

The reduction in floor space utilized is measured by product line. This is typically accomplished by mapping the process and measuring the physical distance the product travels from first step to last step in the production process. Measure monthly and display trend by product line.

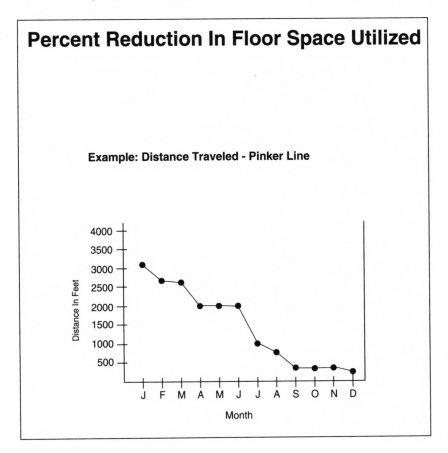

Percent Reduction In Floor Space Utilized

Example: Distance Traveled - Pinker Line

61

Flexibility

1) Percent reduction in cycle time.

The reduction in cycle time is measured by product line. The measurement is the ratio calculated by dividing actual cycle time by the theoretical cycle time. Actual cycle time is normally based on average work in process throughput time. Theoretical cycle time is based on value add time for a lot size of one. It contains no inspections, setup or queue time. Both work in process and administrative cycle time should be measured. Measure monthly and display trend.

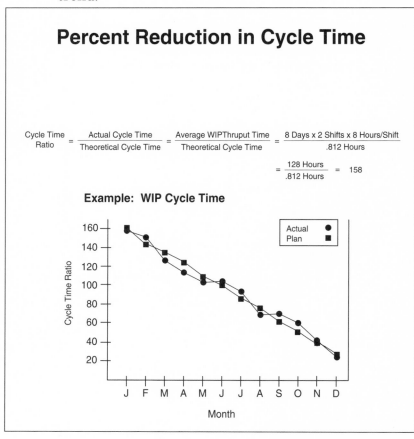

2) Percent reduction in setup time.

Reduction in setup or changeover of the equipment or production line is an important measure of continuous improvement and flexibility. The measure can be daily, weekly or monthly, depending on the current frequency of changeover. Measure by machine and display on a trend line.

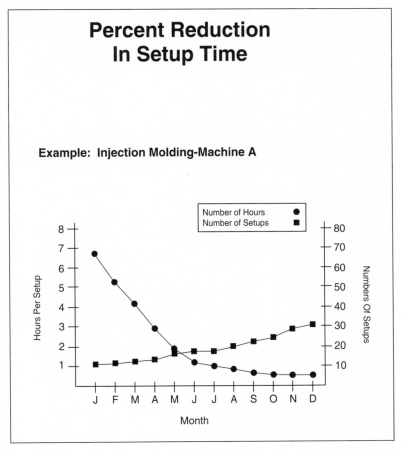

63

3) *Percent reduction in lot / batch size.*

The measurement of lot/batch size reduction measures the trend in reduction of lot sizes. It is usually measured monthly as average lot size by production process.

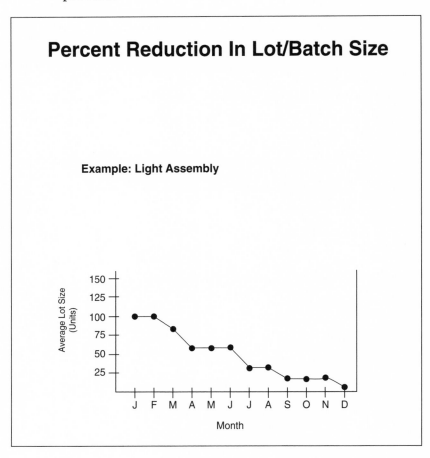

Percent Reduction In Lot/Batch Size

Example: Light Assembly

4) *Percent increase in number of jobs mastered per employee.*

The purpose of increasing the number of jobs mastered per employee is not only for improvement of flexibility, but to help facilitate the habit of improvement. This is accomplished by continuously providing a "different set of eyes" engaged in the process. Most companies involve hourly workers in the development of qualifications for certification and deciding whether someone is to be certified. Display is normally in the work area, showing each individual and their number of jobs mastered.

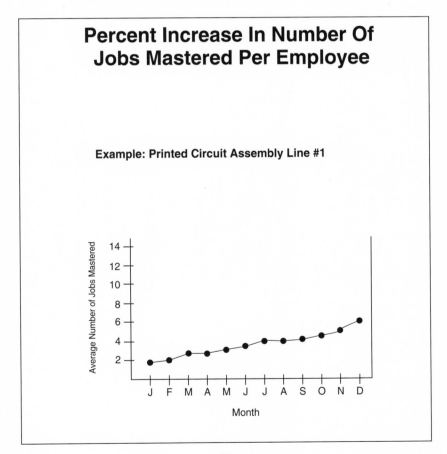

Percent Increase In Number Of Jobs Mastered Per Employee

Example: Printed Circuit Assembly Line #1

5) *Percent increase in common materials used per product.*

Measurement would be at the time of design release and is total common materials (current active items) divided by total materials by product. Measure relative to goals set for standardization at the time design was initiated.

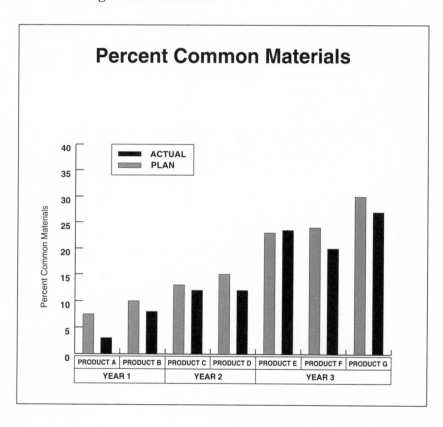

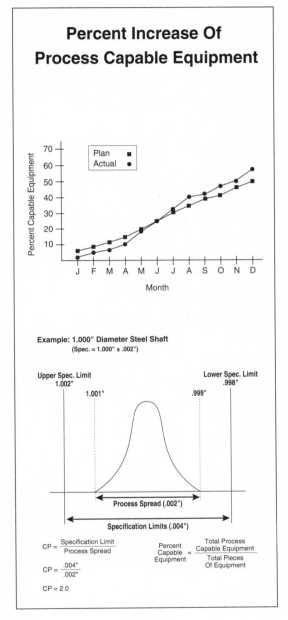

Percent Increase Of Process Capable Equipment

Example: 1.000" Diameter Steel Shaft
(Spec. = 1.000" ± .002")

Upper Spec. Limit 1.002"

Lower Spec. Limit .998"

1.001"

.999"

Process Spread (.002")

Specification Limits (.004")

$$CP = \frac{Specification\ Limit}{Process\ Spread}$$

$$CP = \frac{.004"}{.002"}$$

$$CP = 2.0$$

$$Percent\ Capable\ Equipment = \frac{Total\ Process\ Capable\ Equipment}{Total\ Pieces\ Of\ Equipment}$$

Reliability

1) Percent increase of process capable equipment.

The first step must be to establish that the equipment is statistically in control. Then measure process capability. The measure is percent of machines or processes at CP = 2.0. CP is the specifications width (tolerance) divided by the process spread (+/- 3 sigma). Measure number of machines in the department divided by the number of machines capable of meeting this standard.

2) *Percent increase in overall equipment effectiveness.*

Machine effectiveness is availability (hours running divided by scheduled run hours) times performance (actual machine cycle or rate divided by theoretical machine cycle or rate) times rate of quality product (good material divided by total material run).

Measurement is for three purposes:

1) Does the machine run all of the time scheduled?

2) Is the equipment fit for use to be run at the speed it was designed to run at?

3) Does the equipment produce quality material?

Measure progress on run charts and summarize by department and machine monthly.

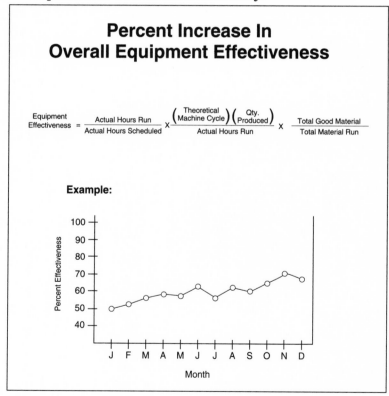

3) *Percent reduction in warranty costs.*

Measure and track monthly by product line in dollars percent of sales and as percent of operating cost. Utilize trend charts.

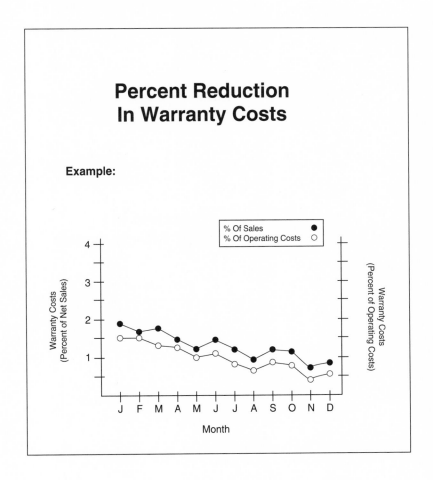

Percent Reduction
In Warranty Costs

Example:

4) *Percent reduction in engineering changes.*

Measure by comparing a series of new products released to manufacturing. The measure is for right first time or quality of the release. Depending upon the frequency of new product introduction, the measurement can be monthly by product line on a trend line.

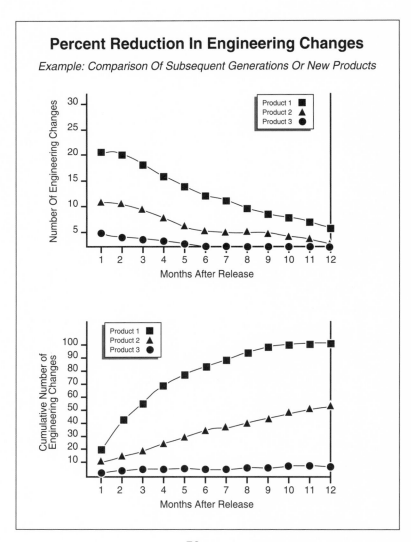

Percent Reduction In Engineering Changes

Example: Comparison Of Subsequent Generations Or New Products

5) *Percent increase in on-time delivery.*

Measurement is whether the product was shipped to the customer in the time frame promised.

Actual measurement is orders shipped on-time divided by total orders shipped.

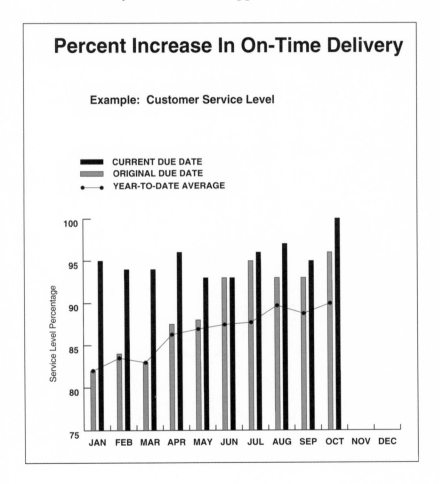

Percent Increase In On-Time Delivery

Example: Customer Service Level

Innovation

1) Reduction in new product introduction lead time.

The measurement indicates your ability to achieve and maintain a competitive advantage by introducing more new products, faster, at lower cost and more reliable than your competitors. It is calculated as the total elapsed time in weeks from concept to release for volume production. It should be measured by product in total as well as by individual phase of the process (Concept, Design, Prototype, Pilot, Release To Volume Production).

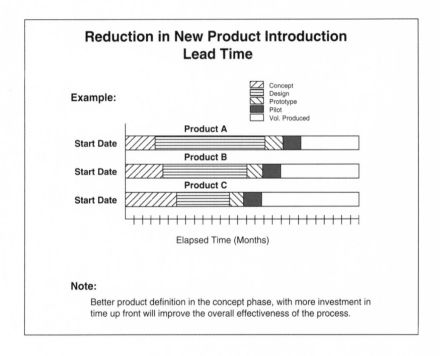

Reduction in New Product Introduction Lead Time

Example:

Concept
Design
Prototype
Pilot
Vol. Produced

Product A

Start Date

Product B

Start Date

Product C

Start Date

Elapsed Time (Months)

Note:

Better product definition in the concept phase, with more investment in time up front will improve the overall effectiveness of the process.

2) *New product sales revenue as a percent of total sales revenue.*

Determine optimum levels required for your products and markets, incorporate into your strategic plans and annual business plans and measure performance depicted on trend charts.

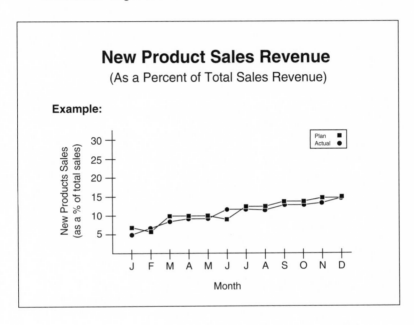

New Product Sales Revenue

(As a Percent of Total Sales Revenue)

Example:

3) Number of new patents granted.

Measurement is a key indicator of the level of creativity and innovation in the entire company. It pertains to older products, existing products (extending their life cycles through such things as addition of new features and options), and processes used to develop, produce, administer market and sell your products and services. It is measured quarterly and/or annually and depicted on trend charts.

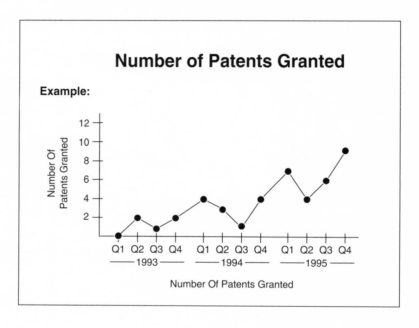

4) *Customer perception of the company as a leader in innovation.*

The focus must be both internal (your employees are your customers as well as customers and suppliers to each other) and external.

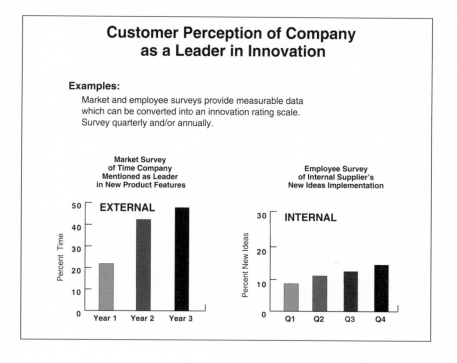

Customer Perception of Company as a Leader in Innovation

Examples:

Market and employee surveys provide measurable data which can be converted into an innovation rating scale. Survey quarterly and/or annually.

Market Survey of Time Company Mentioned as Leader in New Product Features — EXTERNAL

Employee Survey of Internal Supplier's New Ideas Implementation — INTERNAL

5) *Percent of management time spent on leading or fostering innovation.*

This is measured individually from personal calendars and estimates, summarized weekly and reported monthly. It is depicted on trend charts. Sometimes a more formal tour, called work sampling, can be used where individuals record their activity, based on a random signal and based on these samples estimating the percentage.

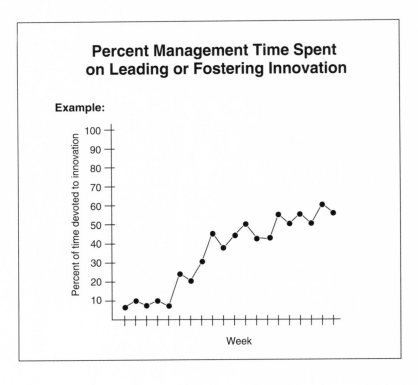

WORLD CLASS PERFORMANCE HISTORY

FUNCTIONAL AREA		JAN.	FEB.	MAR.	APR.	MAY	JUNE	JULY	AUG.	SEPT.	OCT.	NOV.	DEC.
QUALITY	% reduction in total cost of quality												
	% reduction in defect												
	% of certified suppliers												
	% reduction in supplier base												
	% reduction in time between defect occurrence, detection and correction												
COST	% increase inventory turnover												
	% reduction in data transactions												
	% increase in material shipped to point of use by supplier												
	% increase in output $ per employee												
	% reduction in floor space utilized												
FLEXIBILITY	% reduction in cycle time												
	% reduction in setup time												
	% reduction in lot/batch size												
	% increase number of jobs mastered per employee												
	% increase in common materials used per product												
RELIABILITY	% increase of process capable equipment												
	% increase in overall equipment effectiveness												
	% reduction in warrantee costs												
	% reduction in engineering changes												
	% increase in on-time delivery												
INNOVATION	% reduction in new product introduction lead time												
	% increase in new product sales revenue as a percent of total sales revenue												
	number of new patents granted												
	customer perception of the company as a leader in innovation												
	% of management time spent on leading or fostering innovation												

Recommended Professional Societies for Continued Learning

Association for Manufacturing Excellence
380 West Palatine Road
Wheeling, Illinois 60090

American Society for Quality Control
P.O. Box 3005
Milwaukee, Wisconsin 53201-3005

American Production and Inventory Control Society
(APICS)
500 West Annandale Road
Falls Church, Virginia 22046-4274

List of Graphics

Acknowledgments

David W. Buker, Inc. wishes to acknowledge:

1. Richard Schonberger who coined the term World Class Manufacturing. *World Class Manufacturing: The Lessons of Simplicity Applied,* by Richard Schonberger. Free Press Division of MacMillan, Inc. 1986

2. *Characteristics of World Class Manufacturers, Production and Inventory Management Journal,* Third Quarter 1991. Authors: Joel D. Wisner, Ph.D., Department of Management, UNLV, Las Vegas, Nevada and Stanley E. Fawcett, Ph.D., Graduate School of Business Administration, Michigan State University, East Lansing, Michigan